# The Anti-Boredom Activity Book

Silver Dolphin

**Silver Dolphin Books**

An imprint of Printers Row Publishing Group
A division of Readerlink Distribution Services, LLC
10350 Barnes Canyon Road, Suite 100, San Diego, CA 92121
www.silverdolphinbooks.com

Illustrated by Adrian Barclay, Chris Dickason, Clive Goodyer, Emily Golden Twomey, Daniel Limon, Paul Moran, Andy Rowland

Printers Row Publishing Group is a division of Readerlink Distribution Services, LLC. Silver Dolphin Books is a registered trademark of Readerlink Distribution Services, LLC.

All notations of errors or omissions should be addressed to Silver Dolphin Books, Editorial Department, at the above address. All other correspondence (author inquiries, permissions) concerning the content of this book should be addressed to:

Michael O'Mara Books Ltd
9 Lion Yard
Tremadoc Road
London, UK SW47NQ

ISBN: 978-1-68412-653-8

Manufactured, printed, and assembled in Shenzhen, China.
RRD/03/19
23 22 21 20 19  1 2 3 4 5

# GONE FISHING

Complete the maze to put the anchor to the bottom of the sea.

Answer on page 124

3

# Hoot, hoot!

Try copying this wise owl onto the next page, using the grid for help.

Then color him in, of course!

# GO WILD

Follow the color key to bring these wild animals to life.

COLOR IN THE
GREAT BARRIER REEF

Answer on page 124

# CONNECT THE DOTS

See what's hiding beneath the waves.

# FISH FOR DINNER

Add more fish to complete this bait ball.

Give the sleeping lizards colorful stripes.

Find the spotted frogs and fill them in with crazy colors.

# DESIGN YOUR OWN STAMPS

# SEA VOYAGE

Complete the maze to take the diver to the bottom of the sea.

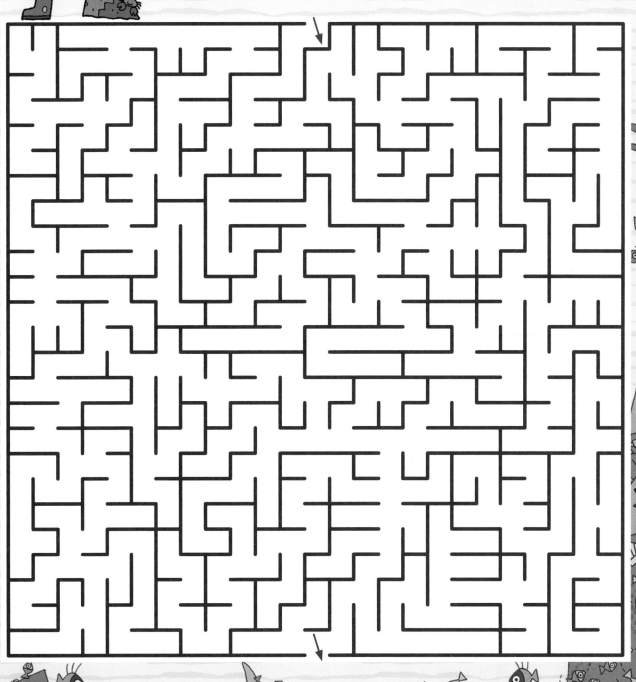

Answer on page 124

# IN TOO DEEP

Draw what you think could be lurking in the darkness.

# SEARCH CRAZY

Spot all the things on the list and color them in as you go.
Once you've finished there will only be one thing left.
What is it?

5 flowers
3 ice cream cones
2 roller skates
4 fish
3 balloons
4 carrots
7 birds
3 teapots
6 apples
8 stars
4 lightning bolts
2 cats
6 hatching dragons
8 doughnuts
4 hamsters
4 bananas
4 cupcakes

Answer on page 125

# UNDER THE SEA

1 = light blue   2 = dark blue   3 = light green   4 = dark green

5 = red   6 = orange   7 = yellow   8 = pink   9 = gray

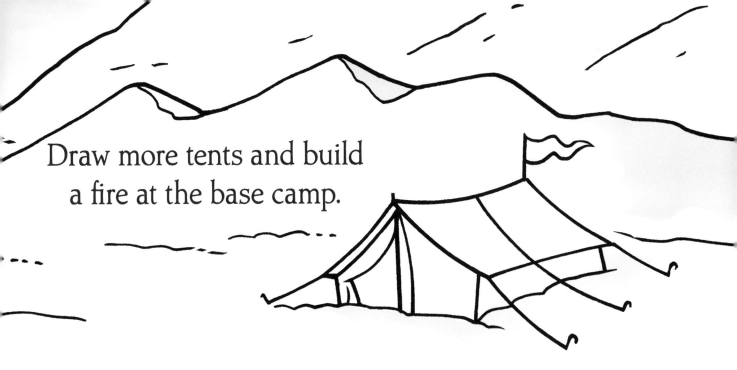

Draw more tents and build
a fire at the base camp.

# HAPPY HERD

Connect the dots to reveal a BIG picture.

29

# PICTURE PUZZLER

Tackle these picture puzzles. The first one is a brain-teaser, the second one is a brain-buster!

Complete this grid so that the four different pictures shown below appear in every row, in every column, and in each outlined block of four squares.

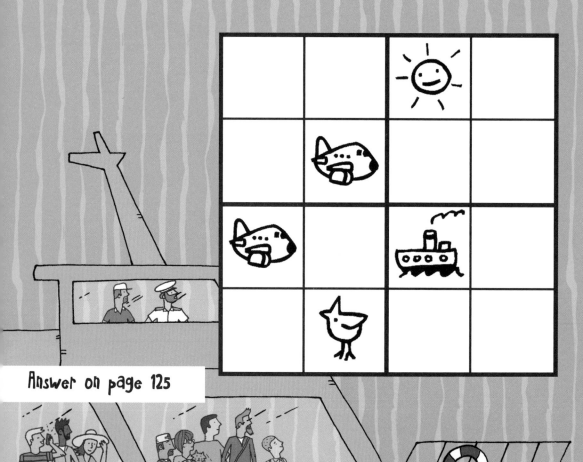

Answer on page 125

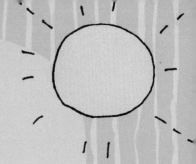

# READY FOR A HARDER PUZZLE?

Try completing the grid below so the nine different pictures shown at the bottom of the page appear in every row, every column, and in each outlined block of nine squares.

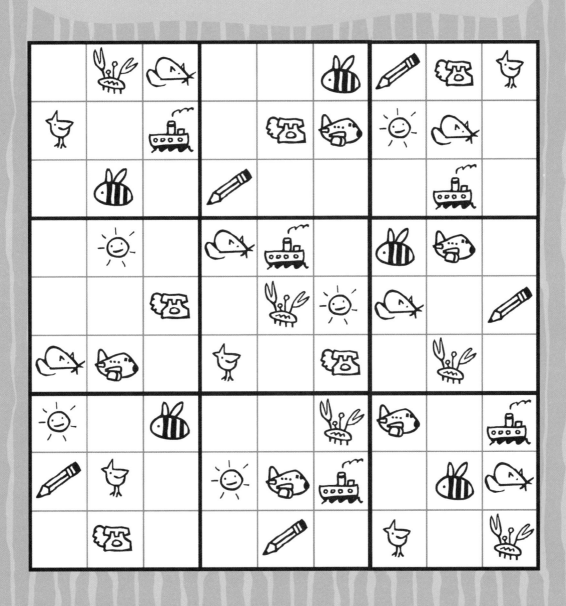

Answer on page 125

# COLOR SCRAMBLE

To color the picture opposite you must follow the
number code below, but first you must unscramble
the letters of each color to reveal what it is.

E R D     <u>RED</u>     = 1

U R P P E L     <u>PURPLE</u> = 2

E L B U     <u>BLUE</u>     = 3

W E L L Y O     <u>YELLOW</u> = 4

R E N G E     <u>GREEN</u> = 5

R A G N E O     <u>ORANGE</u> = 6

You've cracked it! Now complete the
color-by-numbers picture.

Answer on page 125

# MASTER BUILDER

Below is a picture of the Taj Mahal, a beautiful building in India. Every year, millions of tourists flock to admire it. Using the squares in the grid below to help you, can you copy it?

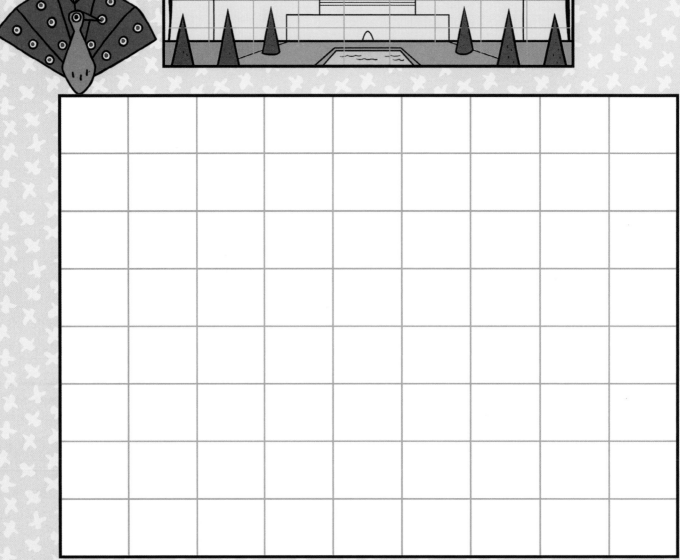

35

# AHOY, MATEY!

Connect the dots to complete the treasure map

# FOSSIL FUN

What types of fossils have been found on the beach?

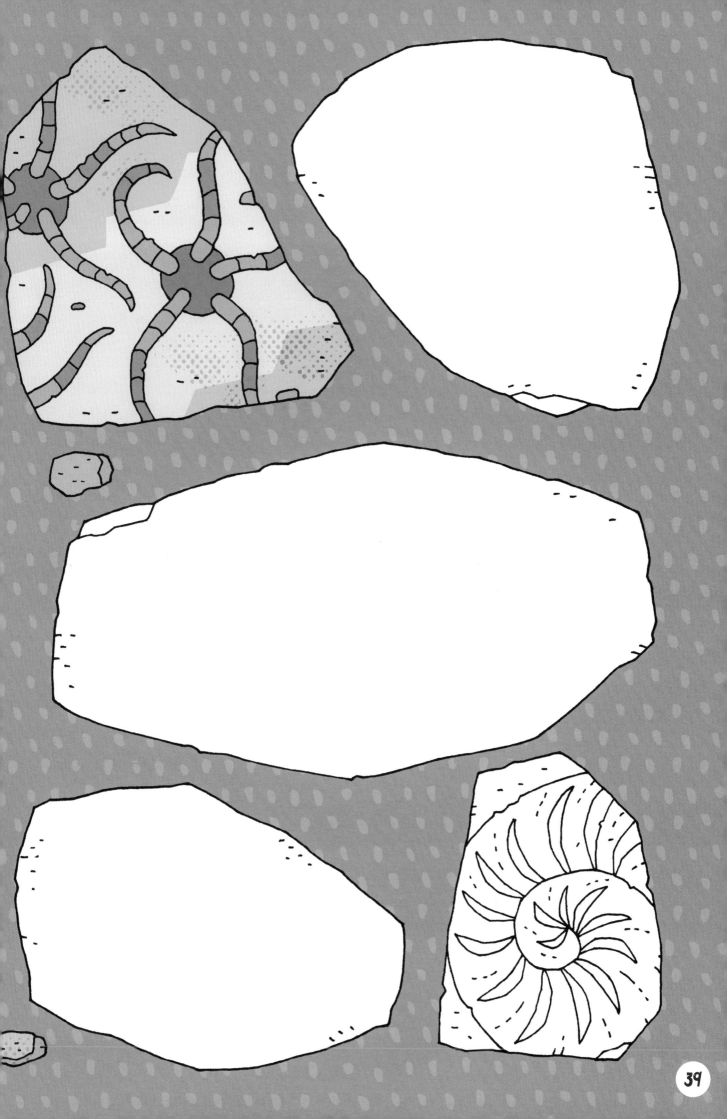

Clever kids to the rescue! Fill in each section in the same color as the dot.

# ISLAND FUN

Draw and color all the things you would find on your dream island.

# COLOR CHALLENGE

Each owl in this midnight forest has a twin.
Find each pair and color them so they are the same.

# HOME SWEET HOME

1 = yellow   2 = red   3 = pink   4 = orange   5 = light blue   6 = dark blue

# SILLY SEA CREATURES

1 = red   2 = orange   3 = yellow   4 = pink   5 = purple   6 = blue

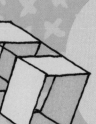

# PICTURE POSTCARDS

Connect the dots to create postcards to send to friends. Make sure you color them in.

# DESERT DOTS

Connect the dots and add some
color to this Egyptian scene.

Color in all of the four-spined dinosaurs.

# MACHINE MAYHEM

Max and Penelope have forgotten where they parked their vehicle in the hover park. Can you help them find it?

**Now design your own crazy vehicle.**

Once you know which box makes the robot, color him in below.

# TREASURE

Color the chest and fill it with treasures.

Add more islands and details to this treasure map.

# CRAZY CREATURES

**Name:** Max Quackbug

**Superpower:** Can turn water into chocolate milkshake

**Name:** The Stompjangler

**Superpower:** With the stomp of her foot she can shrink to the size of her hat

**Name:**

**Superpower:**

**Name:**

**Superpower:**

The creatures that live on Planet Ahh-Boredom are mega mash-up creations. They can do all sorts of cool things. and give them funny names and superpowers.

**Name:** Penelope Snout-foot

**Superpower:** Burps candy

**Name:** Lord Sliverfluff

**Superpower:** Extreme octo-knitting

**Name:**

**Superpower:**

**Name:**

**Superpower:**

# MARKET TRADE

Complete the maze to help the traders
collect their goods to sell.

Answer on page 126

Connect the dots to see who's standing tall.

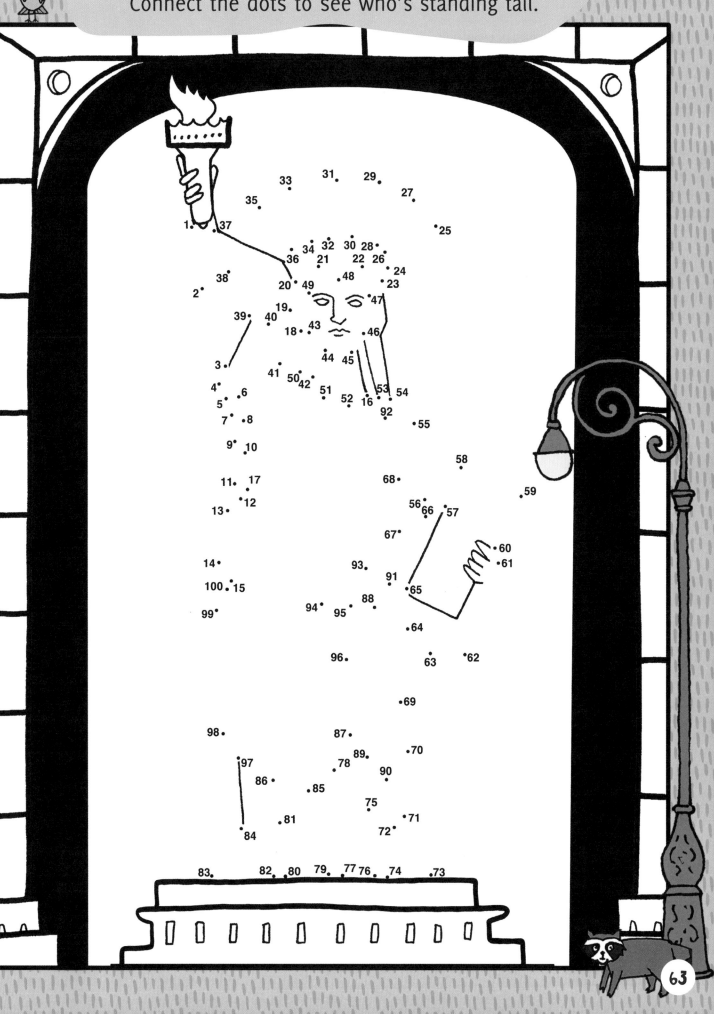

Each fish and each shell has an identical twin. Can you find it and color it in to match?

Spot all the seahorses and color them orange and yellow.

# HOME SWEET HOME

There's never a boring moment on Planet Anti-Boredom. Can you spot **10** differences between the two houses?

Answer on page 126

What's happening on this cruise ship? Fill it in with more people and activities.

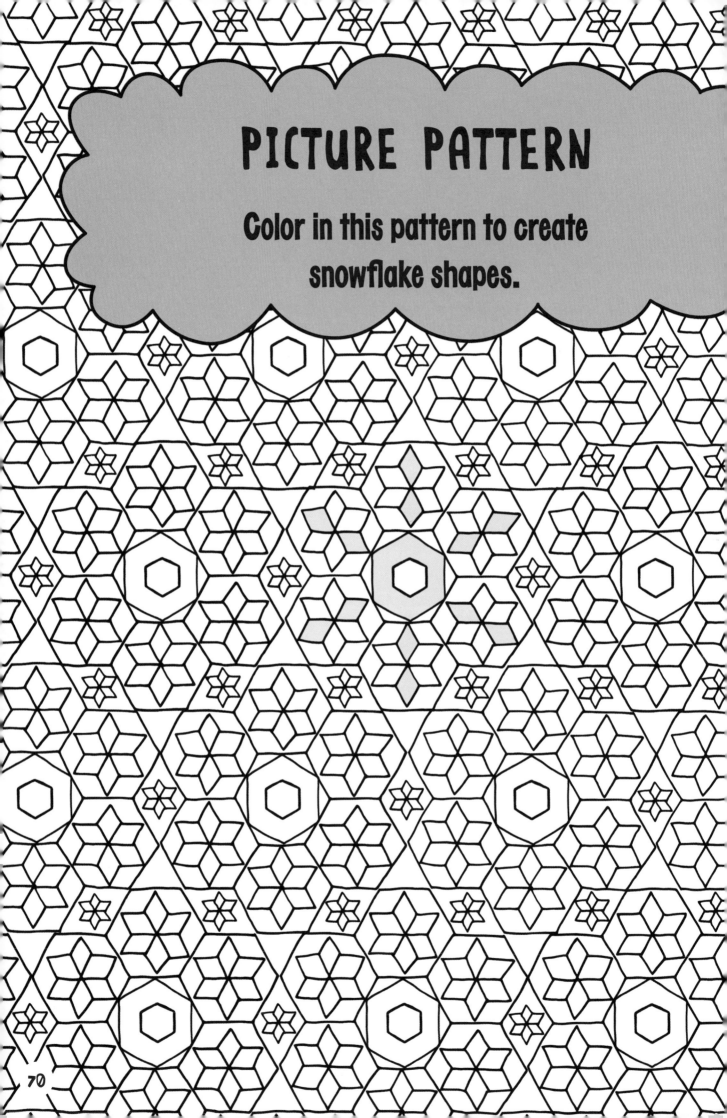

# PICTURE PATTERN

Color in this pattern to create snowflake shapes.

71

# COLOR IN THE SAVANNA

Find all the three-horned monsters and color them in.

# SPOT THE DIFFERENCES

Can you find the eight differences
between these two scenes?

Answer on page 126

# WATER-SKI

Which two water-skiers are
no longer connected to boats?

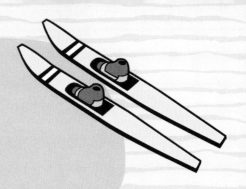

Answer on page 127

# BOLT TO BOLT

What are they making in the factory today? Connect the nuts and bolts to find out.

81

# SEAHORSE FAMILY

1 = blue   2 = pink   3 = orange   4 = yellow

5 = purple   6 = red   7 = green

Decorate and color the turtle's shell.

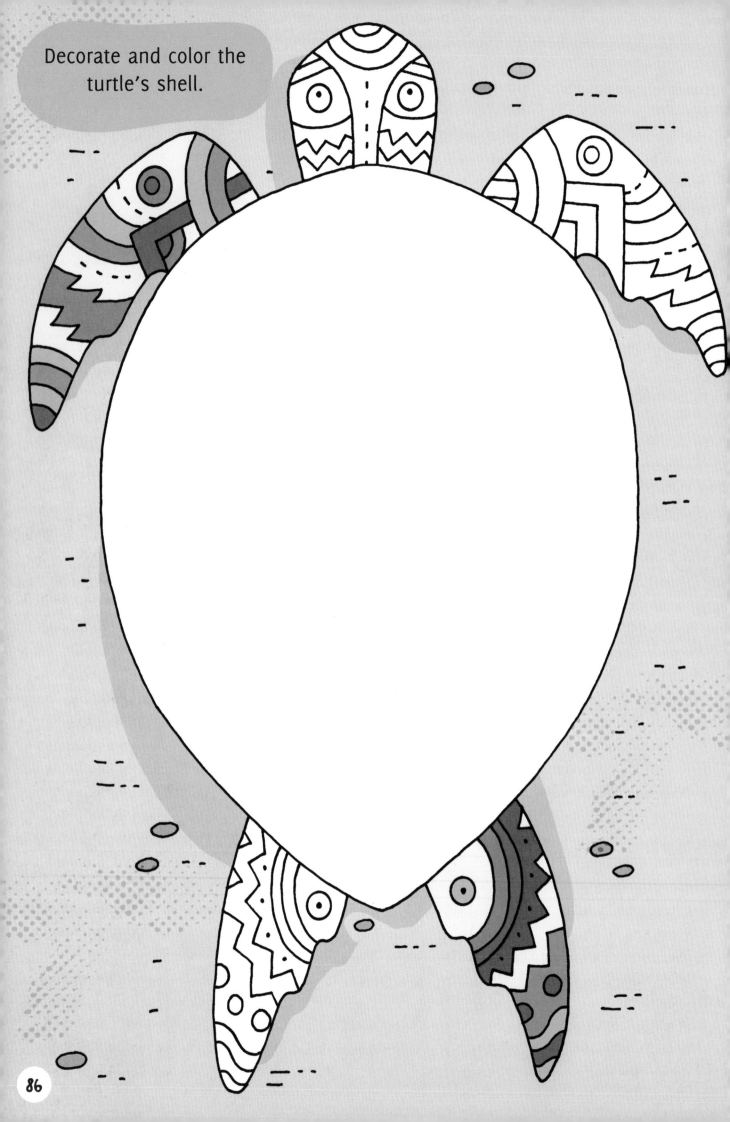

# SPOT THE DIFFERENCES

Can you find the six differences
between these two scenes?

Answer on page 127

# SHELL-TASTIC

Decorate these shells with eye-catching patterns.

# WINDOW WATCH

What's going on outside the window?

# TIME TO EXPLORE!

What has the explorer discovered
in the rain forest?

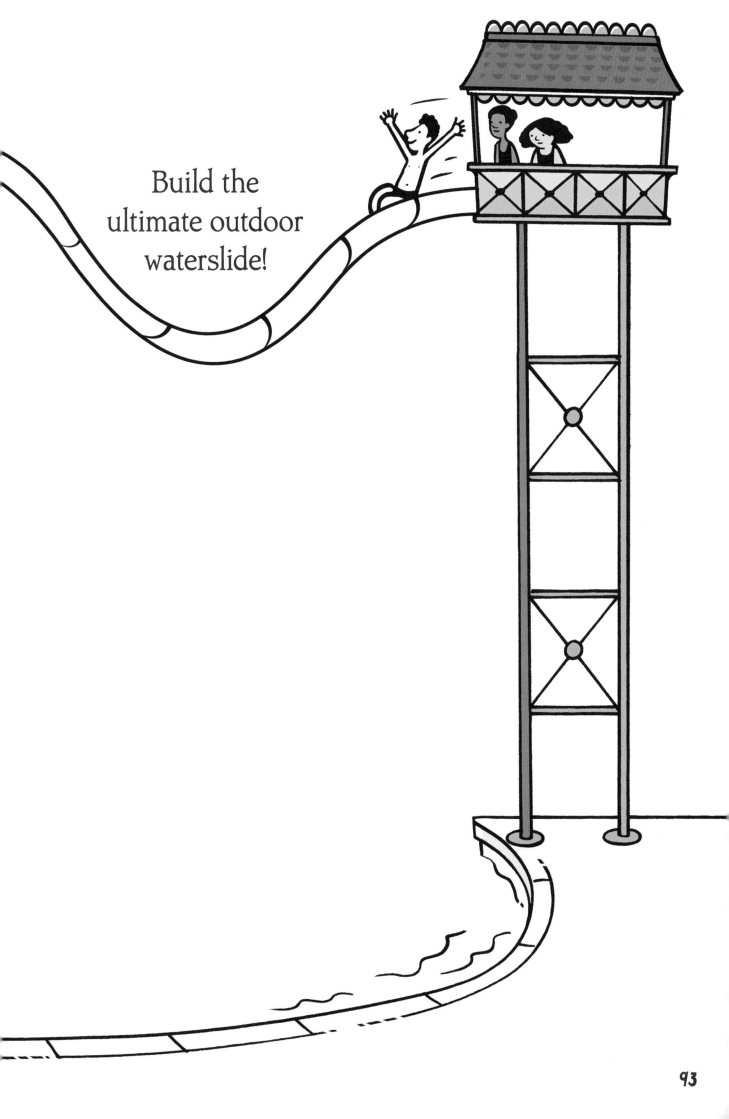

Build the ultimate outdoor waterslide!

# THINGS THAT GO

Kick-start your brain into gear
with these fun puzzles.

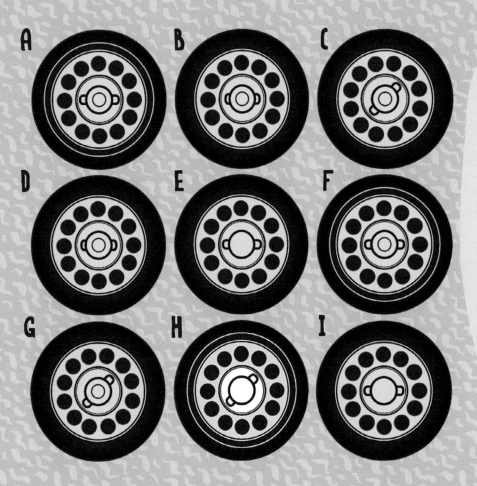

## WHICH WHEELS?

These nine wheels look very similar, but there are four matching pairs and one wheel that is not like any other.

Can you pick out the four pairs and spot the wheel that is the odd one out?

## BITS 'N' PIECES

Only one of the boxes below contains all the bits needed to make this picture of a plane. Which box includes all the pieces?

Answers on page 127

# PUZZLE CITY

## CAPITAL CITY CHECKLIST

Match the capital cities to the countries in which they are found. The first one has been done for you to get you started.

| | |
|---|---|
| Bangkok | Australia |
| New Delhi | USA |
| Beijing | Thailand |
| Madrid | India |
| Moscow | Russia |
| Berlin | China |
| Paris | France |
| Washington, DC | Spain |
| Canberra | Germany |

## AROUND THE BLOCK

Follow the directions below and see where you would end up.

Turn right out of garage A and take the first right. Turn right again, then take the first left. Take the second right, then turn left and then take the first left.

Which garage do you end up in, B or C?

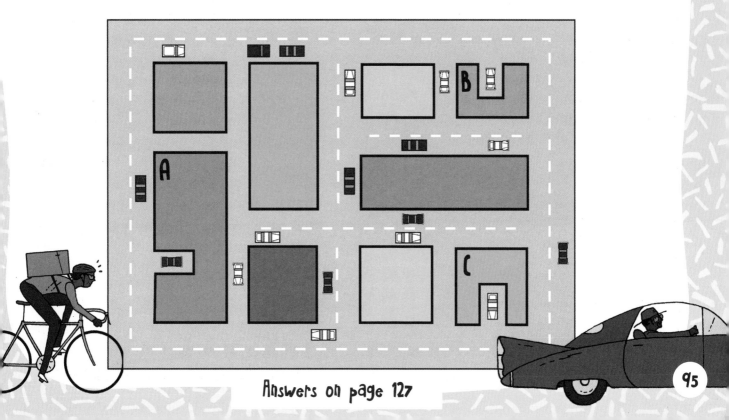

# COLOR SPOT-TASTIC

Color the patches with dots to
reveal an animal picture below.

# YOUR TURN

**Draw your own sea creature
in the space below.**

# Freaky Food Menu

Feast your eyes on these funny foods and complete
the menu with your own crazy dishes.

### Starter:

Banana and broccoli soup

**OR**

.................................................................................................

### Main Course:

Chicken lollipops served with fizzy potato and fudge peas

**OR**

.................................................................................................

### Dessert:

Turnip cake with a sausage-cherry sauce

**OR**

.................................................................................................

Draw a raft in the rushing river.

What creatures are swimming under the snorkeler?

# OUT AT SEA

Follow the color key to reveal the beautiful boats.

Spot all of the dogs wearing collars and color their collars green.

# TEEPEE TENTS

Follow the color key to reveal these quirky tents.

# Connect the dots to reveal a magnificent sandcastle.

Each big bird has an identical little friend. Find each one, then color them in.

# Fill the photos with beautiful sights.

# MAP MAYHEM

When reading a map, combinations of letters and numbers are known as coordinates and refer to locations on the map. To use a coordinate, place your finger on the number given. Trace your finger along the row to the column that matches the letter. In that square you will find the symbol that the coordinates refer to.

**1.** 5A    **2.** 4E    **3.** 1F    **4.** 3B    **5.** 6D    **6.** 3G

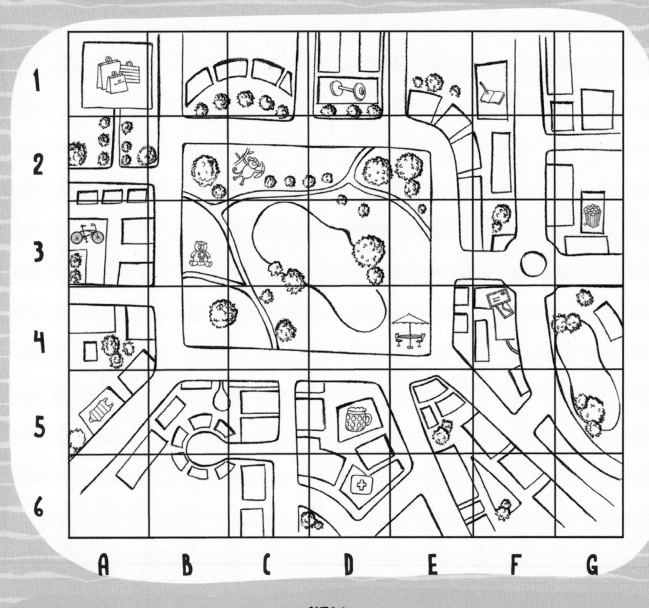

## KEY

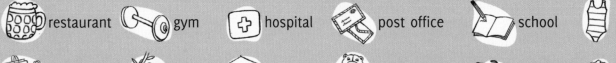

restaurant    gym    hospital    post office    school    swimming pool

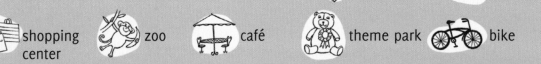

shopping center    zoo    café    theme park    bike    movie theater

Answer on page 128

# ROAD TRIP

## AMERICAN ADVENTURE

You've decided to take a road trip around America. You're going to make three separate car journeys, and one airplane flight. Can you find out which cities you will pass through on each trip described below? Now write down which three cities you will not visit because you don't pass through the squares in which they appear.

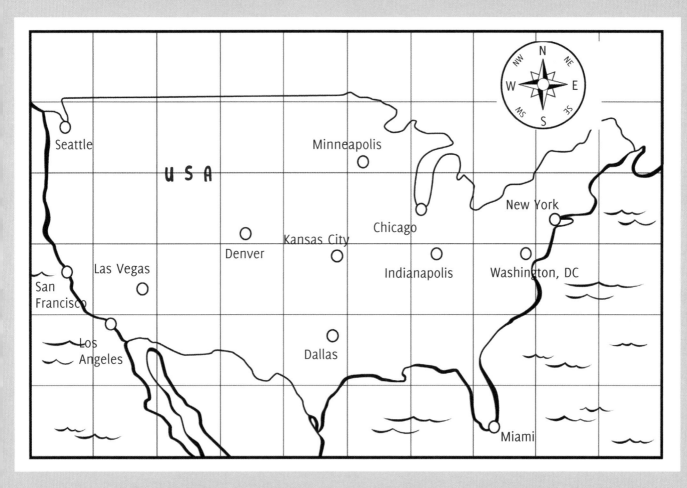

**Trip A.** From New York, you drive one square west, then three squares south, then one square north, then six squares west.

**Trip B.** You fly to Seattle. From there you drive five squares east, then one square south, then one square east, then 5 squares west, then one square south.

**Trip C.** From Las Vegas, you drive one square south, then six squares east, then two squares north and one square east.

Answer on page 128

These clever owls want to visit the museum. Can you find a safe path for them by coloring in the taxis and buses that lead to the museum?

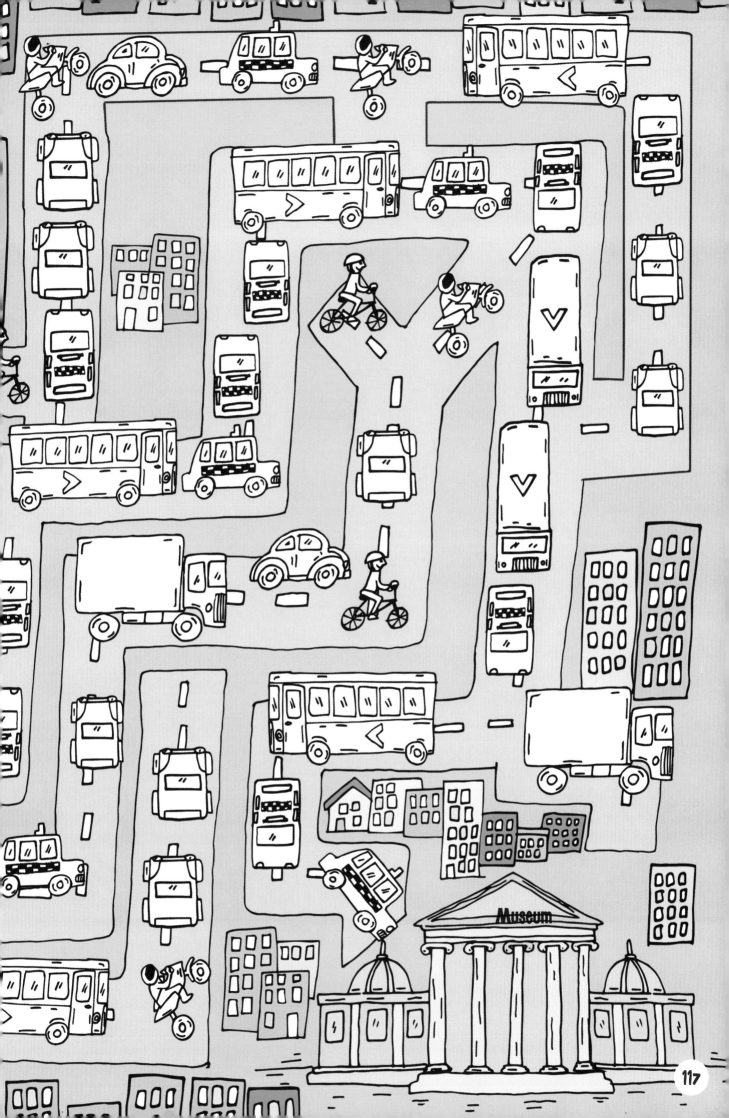

# ON SAFARI

Connect the dots to see what animals
have been spotted on safari.

# SECRET SAFARI

Below is a map of a safari park.
To read it you will need to use coordinates.
A coordinate is a letter and a number that refer to a location on a map. To use a coordinate, place your finger on the letter on the left-hand side of the map. Trace your finger along the row to the column that matches the number. In that square you will find the animal that the coordinate refers to.

Can you find which animals live at the following coordinates?

**1.** D3  **2.** B1  **3.** F3  **4.** C6  **5.** A4  **6.** E6

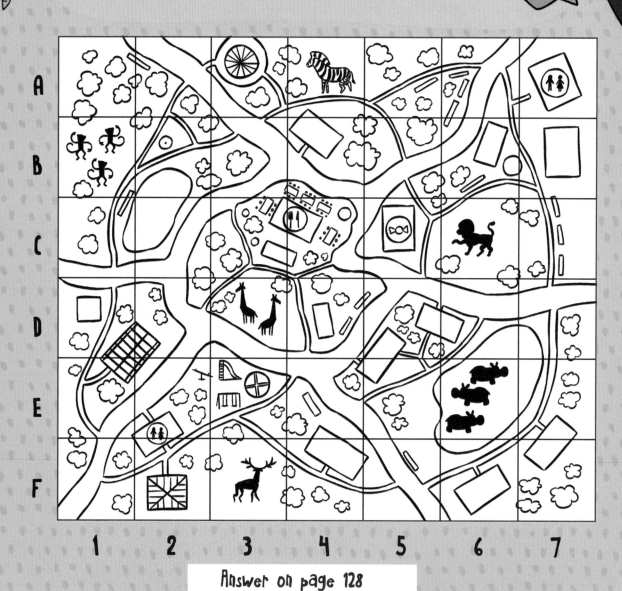

Answer on page 128

# WATER WORLD

Which swimmer will come out of which flume?

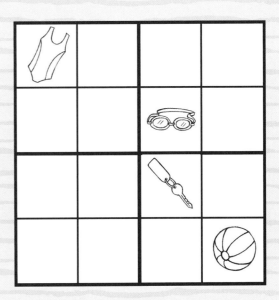

Complete the grid above so that each column, each row, and each of the four larger squares contains only one swimsuit, a beach ball, a locker key, and some goggles.

Using only three straight lines, divide the swimming pool into six sections, with one swimmer and one beach ball in each.

Answers on page 128

# GONE FISHING
## (PAGE 3)

# SPOT THE DIFFERENCES
## (PAGES 10–11)

# SEA VOYAGE
## (PAGE 19)

# SEARCH CRAZY
## (PAGES 22–23)

The last thing left is a dog.

# PICTURE PUZZLER
## (PAGES 30–31)

# COLOR SCRAMBLE
## (PAGES 32–33)

The color code is:
red = 1,
purple = 2,
blue = 3,
yellow = 4,
green = 5,
orange = 6.

# WHICH BOX?
## (PAGES 56–57)

The correct box is C.

## MARKET TRADE
### (PAGE 62)

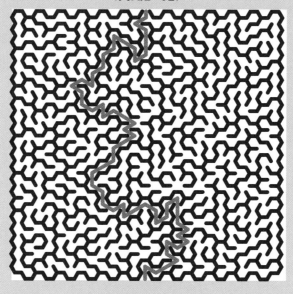

## HOME SWEET HOME
### (PAGES 66–67)

## SPOT THE DIFFERENCES
### (PAGE 76)

## WATER-SKI
## (PAGE 77)

Skiers A and C have
lost their boats.

## SPOT THE DIFFERENCES
## (PAGE 87)

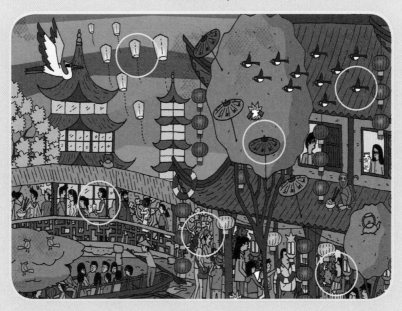

## THINGS THAT GO
## (PAGE 94)

Wheels C and G, B and D, E and
I, and A and F are the same.
Wheel H is unique.

Kit B contains all the bits
to build the plane.

## PUZZLE CITY
## (PAGE 95)

CAPITAL CITY CHECKLIST:
Bangkok = Thailand
New Delhi = India
Beijing = China
Madrid = Spain

Moscow = Russia
Berlin = Germany
Paris = France
Washington, DC = USA
Canberra = Australia

**AROUND THE BLOCK:**
You would end up
in garage C.

# MAP MAYHEM
## (PAGE 114)

5A is a swimming pool.
4E is a café.
1F is a school.
3B is a theme park.
6D is a hospital.
3G is a movie theater.

# ROAD TRIP
## (PAGE 115)

Trip A. New York, Washington, DC, Miami, Dallas, Los Angeles.

Trip B. Seattle, Minneapolis, Chicago, Denver, Las Vegas.

Trip C. Las Vegas, Los Angeles, Dallas, Washington, DC, New York.

You have not visited San Francisco, Kansas City, or Indianapolis.

# SECRET SAFARI
## (PAGE 122)

1. Giraffes, 2. Monkeys, 3. Deer
4. Lion, 5. Zebra, 6. Hippos

# WATER WORLD
## (PAGES 123)

Swimmer A reaches flume 1.
Swimmer B reaches flume 2.
Swimmer C reaches flume 3.
Swimmer D reaches flume 4.